A Kid's Guide to Drawing the Countries of the World™
How to Draw
Italy's
Sights and Symbols

Betsy Dru Tecco

The Rosen Publishing Group's
PowerKids Press™
New York

To Armand, for his "magnifico" love and support

Published in 2004 by The Rosen Publishing Group, Inc.
29 East 21st Street, New York, NY 10010

First Edition

Editor: Frances E. Ruffin
Book Design: Kim Sonsky
Layout Design: Mike Donnellan

Illustration Credits: Cover and inside by Emily Muschinske.
Photo Credits: Cover and title page (hand) by Arlan Dean; cover (Duomo), p. 38 © Jim Zuckerman/CORBIS; p. 5 © Vince Streano/CORBIS; p. 9 © Michael Boys/CORBIS; p. 10 © Dallas and John Heaton/CORBIS; p. 12 © Hulton Archive/Getty Images; p. 13 © Erich Lessing/Art Resource; p. 16 (coin) by Cindy Reiman; p. 20 © Francesco Venturi/CORBIS; p. 22 © philg@mit.edu; p. 24 © Archivo Iconografico, S.A./CORBIS; p. 26 © John Heseltine/CORBIS; p. 28 Doug Mazell/Index Stock Imagery, Inc.; p. 30 © Dallas and John Heaton/CORBIS; p. 32 © Michael S. Yamashita/CORBIS; p. 34 © Owen Franken/CORBIS; p. 36 © Terry Why/Index Stock Imagery, Inc.; p. 40 © Arte and Immagini srl/CORBIS; p. 42 © Sandro Vannini/CORBIS.

Tecco, Betsy Dru.
How to draw Italy's sights and symbols / Betsy Dru Tecco.
    p. cm.—(A kid's guide to drawing the countries of the world)
Summary: Presents step-by-step directions for drawing the flag, Roman mosaics, the Colosseum, a gondola, and other sights and symbols of Italy.
Includes bibliographical references and index.
  ISBN 0-8239-6686-0 (library binding)
1. Drawing—Technique—Juvenile literature. 2. Italy—In art—Juvenile literature. [1. Italy—In art. 2. Drawing—Technique.] I. Title. II. Series.
  NC655 .T36 2004
  743'.93645—dc21

                                                                    2002014777

Manufactured in the United States of America

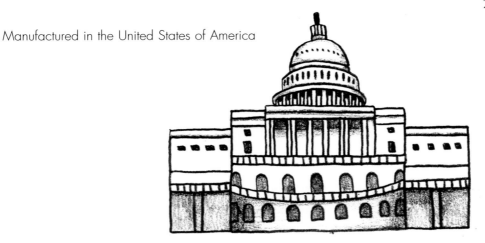

CONTENTS

Let's Draw Italy

Italy is home to more famous works of art than any other place on Earth. The reason for this can be traced to the Renaissance, a movement that brought about new ways of thinking and learning, which started in Italy during the fourteenth century. Some of the greatest works of Renaissance painting, sculpture, and architecture of that time were created by Leonardo da Vinci and Michelangelo Buonarroti. The Renaissance spread to other countries in Europe and lasted for more than 100 years. Many important events happened during the Renaissance, and Italians led the way. Marco Polo, a Venetian man, traveled throughout Asia and wrote the book *A Description of the World*, which raised people's interest in faraway lands. In 1492, Christopher Columbus sailed to North America. America got its name from another Italian explorer, Amerigo Vespucci, who traveled there for the first time in 1497. In 1632, astronomer Galileo Galilei helped to prove that Earth orbits the Sun.

The colonnade, or series of columns, on the left is from the Temple of Saturn. The columns on the right are from the Temple of Vespasian. The remains are part of the Roman Forum, an open space where ancient Romans conducted their business and political affairs.

5

Italy's history is as interesting as its art. The Etruscan people formed Italy's first great civilization about 3,000 years ago. They took control of the small village of Rome, and they built many other towns in Italy. In 509 B.C., they lost power to the Romans, who learned about art, architecture, fashion, and religion from the Etruscans. Over time, the Romans took more control of Etruscan land until they had a huge empire. By the year A.D. 117, the Roman Empire included parts of Europe, Africa, and Asia, lands that are now more than 40 modern countries.

In the third century, the empire was attacked by the Goths, or Lombards, people who lived in what is modern-day Germany. These people wanted the rich land for themselves. The empire slowly broke apart. By the end of the twelfth century, Italy consisted mostly of small regions called city-states. Each city-state had its own political system, run by rich and powerful families. Italy did not form its own kingdom until 1861. Although Italy had a king until the end of World War II, during the war years, fascist Benito Mussolini took power and ruled Italy as a dictator until he was executed in 1945. By

1946, one year after the war ended, the people chose to make Italy a republic. This unified the city-states into one country, making it one of the youngest countries in Europe. Today, Italy has a president and a prime minister.

In this book, you will get to know some of Italy's beautiful sights and symbols and learn about the artists and builders who created them.

You will need the following supplies to draw Italy's sights and symbols:

- A sketch pad
- An eraser
- A number 2 pencil
- A pencil sharpener

These are some of the shapes and drawing terms you need to know to draw Italy's sights and symbols:

— Horizontal line

Oval

Rectangle

Shading

Squiggle

Trapezoid

Triangle

| Vertical line

Wavy line

More About Italy

Many Italians feel more attached to the region where they live than to the country as a whole. Perhaps this is so because Italy was divided for so long. Italy's governmental regions are different from one another. About two-thirds of Italy's nearly 58 million people live in cities. Rome, the capital of Italy, has the largest population, followed by Milan, Naples, and Turin. Most Italians are related to either of two ancient groups, the Romans or the Etruscans.

Farming has always been important to Italians. Yet, because mountains and hills form about two-thirds of the land, about half of the crops must grow on slopes. Olive trees have been growing on the sides of Italy's mountains since ancient times. In fact the country is one of the world's two main producers of olives. Olive oil is a big part of Italian cooking!

Today manufacturing exceeds farming. Fashion is an important Italian trade. Gucci and Giorgio Armani are two famous Italian names in the fashion world. The fine quality of the shoes and clothing they make is valued

A gardener trims the grapevines at La Foce, an estate in Tuscany, Italy, that contains a mansion, or large house, and many gardens.

throughout the world. Italian cars have also become well known. Two of the best-known Italian manufacturers are Fiat and Ferrari.

Italy has few natural resources. Many resources are bought from other countries. The most important mineral resource produced in Italy is natural gas, which is used for energy.

Since World War II, the tourism industry has played a major role in Italy's economy. The country has become a favorite European travel destination because it offers a wide choice of historical and modern-day attractions.

Italy is also a country of lovely sights and sounds. Among the sights are the many sculptures, homes, and buildings that are made of marble. Italy is the world's leading producer of marble. Some of Italy's lovely sounds come from the music of opera. Opera is a drama that is performed by singers, an orchestra, and often dancers. The first opera, Monteverdi's *Orfeo*, was performed in Italy in 1607. Today, Luciano Pavarotti is just one of many world-famous Italian opera singers.

Vacationers from around the world enjoy the sea, sun, and sand of the beaches along the Amalfi Coast in southern Italy.

The Artist Canaletto

Giovanni Antonio
Canaletto

The Italian painter Canaletto was born Giovanni Antonio Canal in Venice in 1697. His father, Bernardo Canal, was also an artist. Both Canaletto and his father painted stage scenery for theaters. While working at this job, Canaletto met artists in Rome who painted in the *vedutismo* style, an Italian style of painting that was very popular in the eighteenth century. Paintings in this style look real, almost as if they are photographs.

Canaletto became a leading master of *vedute*, and Venice was his favorite subject to paint. The Rialto Bridge in Venice was a special source of inspiration for Canaletto. He made many paintings and drawings of this beautiful bridge and the canal flowing below it.

The people who bought Canaletto's paintings were mostly English noblemen. They hired him to paint scenery that they had seen during their visits to Italy. His paintings were like large, expensive postcards that they could take home to England. For a while, Canaletto worked in England, painting scenes of

London and of the country homes of his favorite buyers. However, Canaletto's paintings of Venice and Rome were his greatest masterpieces.

He also created imaginary views known as caprichos, which comes from the Italian word *capriccio*, meaning "fancy." In these works, Canaletto drew together scenes from two different places. For instance, he would paint the ruins of ancient Rome along the canal in Venice. In recognition of his talent, Canaletto was elected to the Venetian Academy of Fine Arts. He died in 1768, at the age of 70.

Canaletto painted the same scene many times, but at different angles and at different times of day. This is one of his oil paintings on canvas, *The Rialto Bridge, Venice*. It measures 47" x 61" (119.4 cm x 155 cm).

Map of Italy

ITALY

Map of the Continent of Europe

Italy is a peninsula, which means it is bordered by water on three sides. These waters include the Adriatic Sea and the Mediterranean Sea. The country has an unusual shape. It looks like a tall boot with a high heel. The boot's toe points to the hilly island of Sicily. North and west of Sicily is another large island, called Sardinia. Both are part of Italy. Smaller Italian islands are scattered along Italy's coast. The total size of Italy is 116,305 square miles (301,228.6 sq km). Italy shares borders with Austria, France, Slovenia, and Switzerland. All are on the continent of Europe. Italy's highest peak, Mont Blanc, shares borders with France and Switzerland. Italy also has many lakes and rivers. The Po, Italy's longest river, flows 405 miles (651.8 km) across northern Italy.

1

Italy is shaped like a boot. Begin your drawing of the map with a half circle that is tilted to the left.

2

From the half circle, draw a long rectangle that stretches out to the right.

3

Add the southern part of Italy with two shapes, shown here, that look like the heel and the toe of a boot.

4

By the toe of the boot, draw the basic curved shape of the island of Sicily.

5

Draw the northern border of Italy inside the half circle. Use a squiggly line.

6

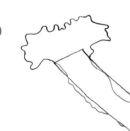

Erase the half circle. Using wavy lines, draw the leg of the boot. Add a small triangle on the island of Sicily to show Mount Etna.

7

Erase extra lines. Use wavy lines to outline southern Italy. Do the same for the island of Sicily. Use the outlines to help you get the curves just right.

8

Erase the outlines. Add a map key and symbols to show more of Italy's special places of interest. Add the island of Sardinia.

☆	Rome
▪	Island of Sicily
Δ	Mount Etna
▲	Mount Vesuvius
+	Vatican City
ϟ	Po River

15

Flag of Italy

When French ruler Napoléon Bonaparte conquered northern Italy in 1796, he brought the French flag with him. It has three vertical stripes of blue, white, and red. Napoléon made the Italian flag similar, but he changed the blue to green. Green was said to be his favorite color. Green and white were also the colors of the army from Milan, Italy. The flag with the green stripe was officially adopted by Italy in 1946, when the monarchy was replaced by a republic.

The Italian Euro

The euro is the common currency for most countries in the European Union. The front of a euro coin shows how much the coin is worth. The back of the coin shows a design that is a symbol of that particular country. This coin shows a detail of *The Birth of Venus*, by fifteenth-century Italian artist Sandro Botticelli.

Flag

1

Draw a rectangle.

2

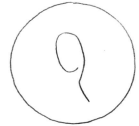

Add a vertical line.

3

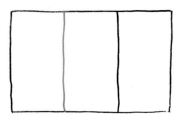

Add another vertical line.

4

Shade your flag using the green, white, and red colors of the Italian flag.

Italian Euro

1

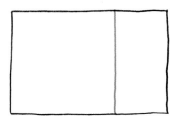

Draw a circle. In the center, add the outline of a woman's head and neck. The head is an oval. The neck is a curved line that extends down from the oval.

2

Draw the details of Venus's face. Add almond-shaped eyes, curved eyebrows, a curved line for the nose, and two lines for her lips.

3

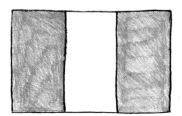

Next draw squiggly lines for her hair, which looks as if it is blowing in the wind. Add the date on the coin, 2002.

4

Draw five-point stars around the outside of the woman's head.

17

Paestum

Almost 3,000 years ago, Greeks began to settle in southern Italy, where they formed a city called Poseidonia. The city is near the modern-day city of Salerno. It was named for Poseidon, the ancient Greek god of the sea. During the sixth century B.C., the Greeks built temples in Poseidonia to honor Poseidon and other gods. The temples had large altars, which are stone tables used during worship. On these altars, the Greeks would sacrifice, or kill, animals to offer as gifts to their gods. Before 400 B.C., Italians from the south captured Poseidonia from the Greeks. In 332 B.C., they changed its name to Paestum. The temples still exist today. The Temple of Neptune, below, which is the Roman name for Poseidon, is one of the best-preserved Greek temples in the world.

1

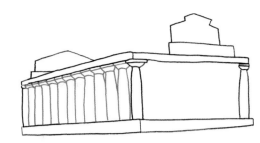

Draw two long, narrow rectangles to begin the temple. Notice that they are a bit wider in the middle, where they meet.

2

Draw two columns using long log shapes, topped by the shapes, as shown. Add a long, thin horizontal rectangle to connect the columns.

3

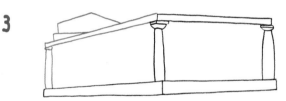

To draw the left side of the temple, add another long, thin rectangle. Draw a column at the far end. At the back of the temple, draw two shapes, as shown, using vertical, horizontal, and diagonal lines.

4

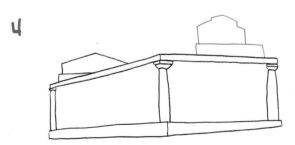

Next draw a pediment, or roof design, in the front of the temple with a rectangle and several lines to form the shape shown here.

5

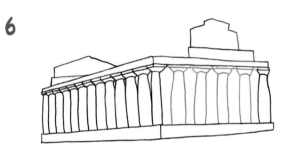

Add a row of columns along the left side of the temple. Draw them using the same shapes that were used to draw the first one.

6

Next add more columns to the front of the temple ruins.

7

Shade the building using squiggly lines to give it the appearance of rough stone. Add dark shading behind the columns, to fill in the space inside the temple.

Sarcophagus of Larthia Seianti

People known as the Etruscans formed Italy's first civilization around 1000 B.C. The Etruscans may have come from the eastern region of the Mediterranean. Religion and life after death were very important to these people. To honor the dead, the Etruscans buried them in stone coffins. A stone coffin is called a sarcophagus. Many of these richly decorated coffins, or sarcophagi, have been found in Italy. They are made from either stone or baked clay called terra-cotta. Women as well as men were respected in the Etruscan society. The sarcophagus of one woman, Larthia Seianti, was found in the Italian town of Chiusi. On the coffin's lid is a statue of the woman, Larthia. She is shown sitting up, and she appears to be putting on her makeup.

Draw a side and an end of the sarcophagus using vertical and diagonal lines. This will make a long and narrow box shape.

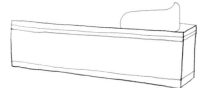

Add four lines to the top and two lines to the bottom of the box. Then add a curved shape to the top of the sarcophagus using wavy lines. This is the pillow on which the woman is leaning. Connect the pillow to the box using a short line.

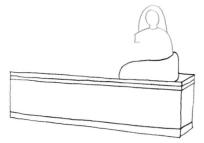

Begin the body of the woman above the pillow by drawing an arch for her veil. Add an oval for her head and curved lines for her neck and shoulders.

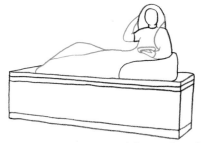

Add her arms using curved lines that bend gracefully. Draw the outline of her robes, which cover her legs. Notice the way one hand is behind her veil. The other hand is holding what may be her makeup.

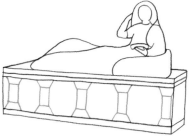

Next add the decoration to the sarcophagus. Draw five columns made with rectangles and diagonal lines, as shown.

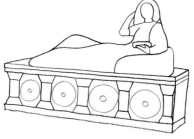

Between the columns, draw four large circles. Add small circles in the center of each large circle.

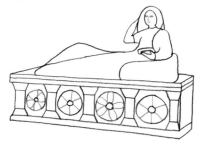

Add features to the statue's face, including almond-shaped eyes. Draw a long L for her nose, and two lines for her mouth. Add several lines to the circles.

Shade your drawing. If you like, you can add curved lines, spirals, and almond shapes inside the circles on the sarcophagus and wavy lines on Larthia's robe.

Bronze Horses

The Basilica di San Marco, or Saint Mark's Basilica, is a beautiful church in Venice. Above its grand entrance are four bronze horses. They may have been created around 300 B.C. by Greek sculptor Lysippus for Alexander the Great. When Alexander died, Roman ruler Octavius took the horses to Rome in about 323 B.C. Constantine the Great, another Roman emperor, moved them to the city of Constantinople, today's Istanbul, Turkey. When the people of Venice conquered Constantinople in 1204, they took the horses to St. Mark's. In 1797, French emperor Napoléon Bonaparte removed the horses from the church and took them to Paris, France. They were returned to Venice in 1815, and are now protected inside the basilica.

1

To draw one of the four horses, draw a circle with a curved line next to it.

2

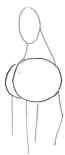

Add two lines for the neck, then add an oval for the head. Draw three straight lines and one bent line to start the legs.

3

Using these lines and basic shapes as guides, draw the horse's right front leg. Notice that there are curves at the knee and ankle. Use two curved lines for the hoof.

4

Notice that the left front leg is made with wavy lines to show the horse's muscles.

5

Draw the rear legs using the same type of lines used to draw the front legs and hooves.

6

Erase extra lines. Draw a breastplate, which is the band at the horse's neck. Then outline the horse's head, and draw two small ears.

7

Add the features to the horse's face. Draw two almond-shaped eyes, hair between the ears, a long curved nose, and a curved cheek.

8

Shade your horse. Notice that the darkest parts are the shadows on the rear legs.

23

The Colosseum

Amphitheaters were first built in ancient Rome. These huge theaters were oval or round structures with rising levels of seats called tiers. The first stone amphitheater was built by Statilius Taurus in 20 B.C. It was destroyed by the Great Fire of Rome in A.D. 64. The Roman Empire's most famous amphitheater, the Colosseum, was completed in Rome in A.D. 80. It was 157 feet (50 m) high, 620 feet (186 m) long, and 513 feet (157 m) wide. It was big enough to seat at least 50,000 people. Many amphitheaters were modeled after the Colosseum. There Romans watched gladiator games, or battles between enslaved men, professional fighters, and even wild animals, who fought and killed one another.

1

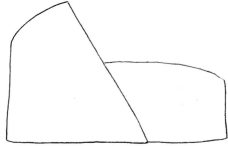

Begin by drawing the two sections of the building. Make these two shapes using curved, diagonal, horizontal, and vertical lines.

2

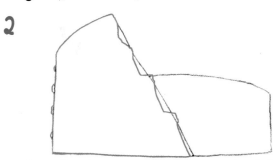

Outline the shape on the left. On the left side, draw four bumps. Make the diagonal line in the middle jagged, almost like stairs.

3

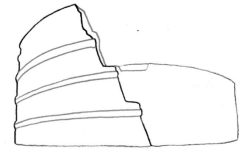

Erase extra lines. Draw three curved double lines from the left side of the building to the right. Draw three small lines in the middle, as shown. Add a line to show the thick wall.

4

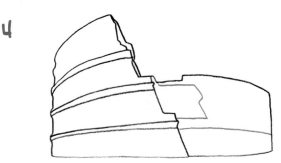

Erase the extra line. Draw a long curving line on the right section of the building. Draw another shape above it, as shown.

5

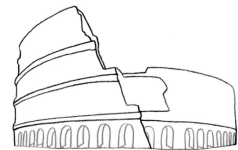

Next draw many arches on the first level. Make the arches wider toward the building's center. Draw another curving line inside of each arch, to show its thick walls.

6

Add arches to the upper levels. Draw two small windows on the top level.

7

Add tiny wavy lines to the top left edge of the building. Draw arches and small windows on the right side of the building.

8

Shade your drawing. Notice that some of the top arches have light coming through and the bottom arches show darker shadows.

25

Roman Mosaics

Mosaic design dates from the fifth century B.C. in Greece. The art form was later adopted by wealthy Romans, who used mosaic work to decorate their homes. Several thousand pieces of colored stone and tile may be used to make one picture or pattern. The pieces may be as small as ⅕ inch (.5 mm) square. To make a mosaic, first a drawing is made. Then the squares are laid one by one in wet plaster to match the drawing.

Many ancient mosaics show everyday scenes. Mosaics in the Piazza Armerina, a large house in Sicily, show hunting and military scenes. It is believed that this house was once owned by the Roman emperor Maximian in the second century B.C.

1

To draw a detail of the mosaic design, let's focus on the boat in which the men are riding. Begin with a long, curving line.

2

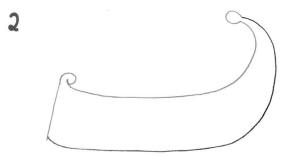

Add a curving line to make the upper part of the boat. Draw round shapes at each end. Add a line for the rear of the boat.

3

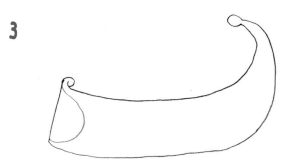

Draw the curve at the end of the boat.

4

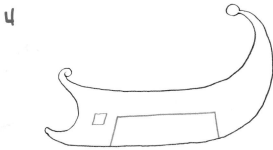

Draw a square just inside the end of the boat and a long shape with three lines in the middle of the boat. Erase extra lines.

5

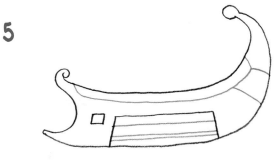

Draw horizontal lines inside the box shape. Add one curved line below the top curved line and two short lines on the right.

6

Draw zigzag lines for decoration on the top of the boat.

7

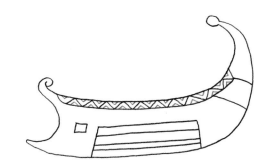

Draw little triangular shapes inside the zigzag lines.

8

Shade your drawing.

Mouth of Truth

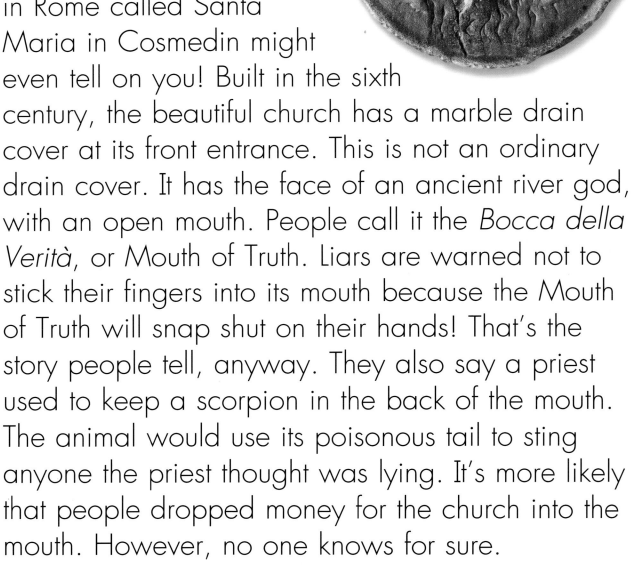

Have you ever told a lie and then worried that you might get caught? A sculpture in a little church in Rome called Santa Maria in Cosmedin might even tell on you! Built in the sixth century, the beautiful church has a marble drain cover at its front entrance. This is not an ordinary drain cover. It has the face of an ancient river god, with an open mouth. People call it the *Bocca della Verità*, or Mouth of Truth. Liars are warned not to stick their fingers into its mouth because the Mouth of Truth will snap shut on their hands! That's the story people tell, anyway. They also say a priest used to keep a scorpion in the back of the mouth. The animal would use its poisonous tail to sting anyone the priest thought was lying. It's more likely that people dropped money for the church into the mouth. However, no one knows for sure.

1

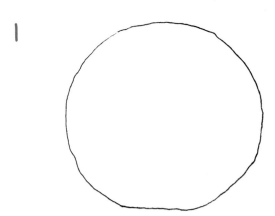

Draw a circle.

2

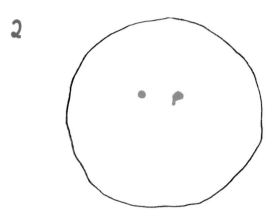

Add two dark dots to begin the eyes. Notice that the eye on the right has a crack in it. The crack makes the eye appear as though it is crying.

3

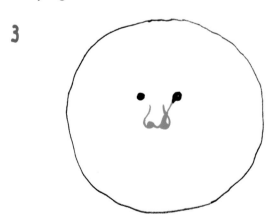

Draw two curved lines to make a nose. Add dark circles for nostrils. Add a dark line from the eye to the right nostril to show that the crack continues through the nose.

4

Shade in a dark oval mouth. Then draw a crack through the mouth and bottom lip.

5

Add shaky curved lines around the face. Add almond-shaped eyes. Draw the mustache using squiggly lines on each side of the mouth. Draw the crack to the outer edge of the circle.

6

Next shade the Mouth of Truth. Use squiggly lines around the face and in the mustache to create the hair.

St. Peter's Basilica

Vatican City has been an independent state within Italy since 1929. The Pope, who is head of the Roman Catholic Church, lives in the Vatican. Inside the Vatican is St. Peter's Basilica, one of the world's largest and most famous churches. Inside the church, there is room for 60,000 people.

In 324, the church was built over the tomb of St. Peter, one of Jesus's 12 disciples, or followers. Pope Nicholas V decided to build a bigger church in 1506. One of the great architects of the time was the artist Michelangelo, who planned the church's grand, 400-foot-high (122-m-high) dome. The church was finally completed in 1626. St. Peter's Basilica is a true wonder of Renaissance architecture.

1

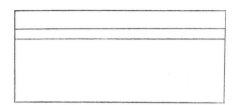

Begin your drawing of St. Peter's Basilica with a large rectangle. Add two horizontal lines.

2

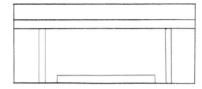

Add two vertical rectangles and one horizontal rectangle.

3

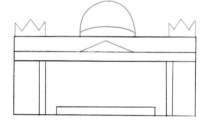

Draw the top of a triangle. Then add two zig-zag shapes on top of the building. Add the dome in the center of the building using two arcs.

4

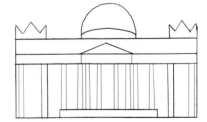

Now, add vertical lines to your drawing.

5

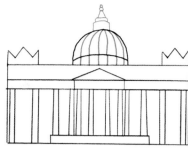

Add arcs to the dome. Then add the five tiny sections on top of the dome. These sections are called the cupola.

6

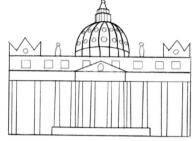

Draw square and circular windows, tiny lines on the cupola, an oval in the center of the large triangle, and two figures on each side of the dome.

7

Add lots of windows to the lower part of the cathedral. Some of the windows have arches at the top.

8

Shade your drawing. Notice the way the shadows are darker inside the windows.

31

Leaning Tower of Pisa

The Leaning Tower of Pisa really leans. In fact, it leans more today than it did when it was first built. In 1173, Bonanno Pisano, a famous sculptor who worked in bronze, began its construction. It was intended to stand alone as a campanile, or bell tower, for a cathedral in Pisa called Il Duomo. Its shallow base rested in sand and clay, not solid earth. By 1274, this base caused the tower to lean, even before the third level was finished. If this eight-story tower stood straight, it would measure about 180 feet (55 m) tall. In centuries since then, work has been done to preserve the tower and to prevent it from falling. It has 200 marble and granite columns, and 293 steps to the top. The Leaning Tower of Pisa may not stand perfectly, but it is a famous symbol of Italy.

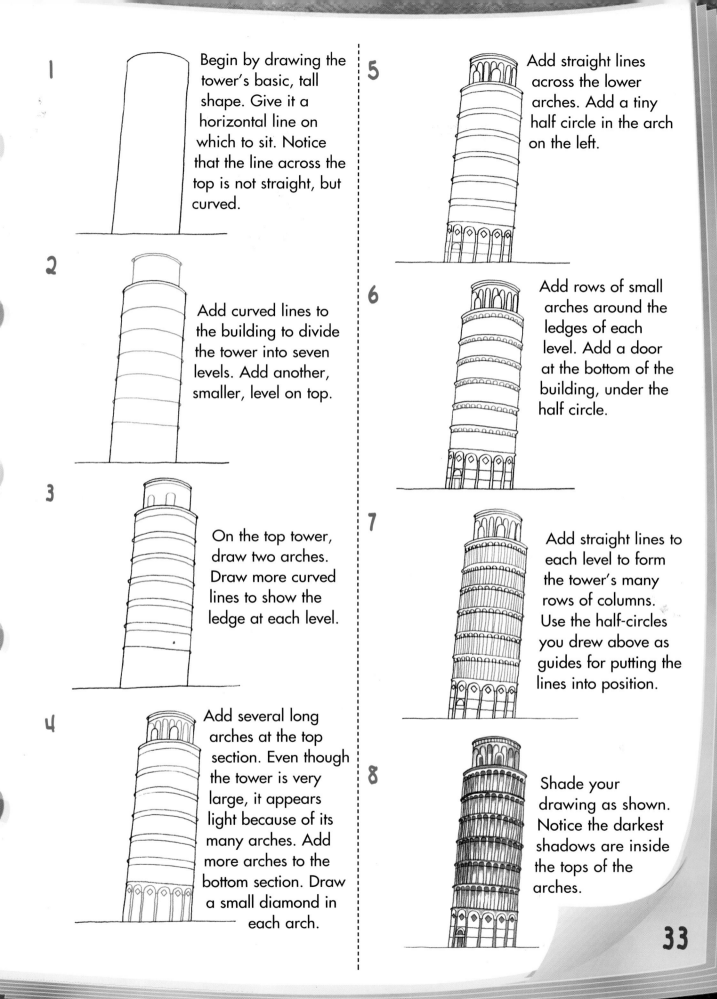

1 Begin by drawing the tower's basic, tall shape. Give it a horizontal line on which to sit. Notice that the line across the top is not straight, but curved.

2 Add curved lines to the building to divide the tower into seven levels. Add another, smaller, level on top.

3 On the top tower, draw two arches. Draw more curved lines to show the ledge at each level.

4 Add several long arches at the top section. Even though the tower is very large, it appears light because of its many arches. Add more arches to the bottom section. Draw a small diamond in each arch.

5 Add straight lines across the lower arches. Add a tiny half circle in the arch on the left.

6 Add rows of small arches around the ledges of each level. Add a door at the bottom of the building, under the half circle.

7 Add straight lines to each level to form the tower's many rows of columns. Use the half-circles you drew above as guides for putting the lines into position.

8 Shade your drawing as shown. Notice the darkest shadows are inside the tops of the arches.

33

Giotto's Campanile and the Duomo

One symbol of Florence is the cathedral, or church, that rises in the center of the city. Its official name is Santa Maria del Fiore, or Saint Mary of the Flowers, but everyone calls it the Duomo. Construction began in 1296. The dome was completed in 1463. It is the city's tallest building and Europe's fourth-largest church. Stripes of green, white, and pink marble cover the outside. On top is a dome, or a cup-shaped roof, made of red-orange tiles. At 296 feet (91 m), it is one of the world's five highest domes.

Next to the Duomo is the finest bell tower in Italy. Giotto's Campanile is named for its creator, Giotto di Bondone. He is considered the first genius of Italian Renaissance art. In 1334, Florence gave Giotto the title of Great Master and made him city architect. He planned the square bell tower, but he died in 1337, before it was completed.

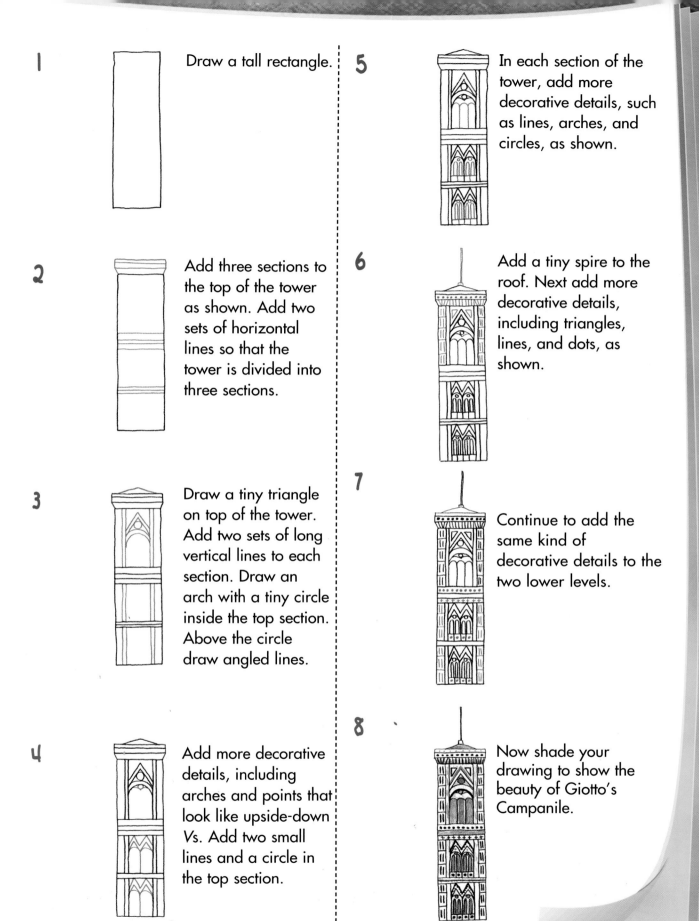

1 Draw a tall rectangle.

2 Add three sections to the top of the tower as shown. Add two sets of horizontal lines so that the tower is divided into three sections.

3 Draw a tiny triangle on top of the tower. Add two sets of long vertical lines to each section. Draw an arch with a tiny circle inside the top section. Above the circle draw angled lines.

4 Add more decorative details, including arches and points that look like upside-down Vs. Add two small lines and a circle in the top section.

5 In each section of the tower, add more decorative details, such as lines, arches, and circles, as shown.

6 Add a tiny spire to the roof. Next add more decorative details, including triangles, lines, and dots, as shown.

7 Continue to add the same kind of decorative details to the two lower levels.

8 Now shade your drawing to show the beauty of Giotto's Campanile.

35

Verrocchio's *David*

According to the Old Testament, a young soldier of Israel named David killed Goliath. Goliath was a 10-foot-tall (3-m-tall) warrior for the Philistines, an ancient people. David shot a small stone from a leather sling into Goliath's head, killing the giant. After that, David became Israel's king as well as a symbol of bravery and freedom. Many artists have made paintings and statues of David. One of the most famous David statues is by Andrea del Verrocchio.

Verrocchio was born Andrea di Cione in 1435, in Florence. He was a leading Italian sculptor and painter during the early Renaissance. Verrocchio's famous bronze statue of David was created in 1470. It stands almost 5 feet (1.5 m) tall. Verrocchio knew a lot about the human body. He carved the strong muscles of David's body and face. David holds Goliath's sword. At his feet is Goliath's head.

1 Begin by sketching an oval head and a cross as a guide for the body.

2 Draw guide lines for one arm hanging straight down and the other arm bent at the elbow with the hand resting on the hip.

3 Draw a line for the hip, which slants down to the right. Then add long lines for legs and feet. Draw a big circle next to David's feet for Goliath's head.

4 Now that you have the basic position of the body, you can draw the main shapes of the body. Begin with the neck, shoulders, and arms. Use curving lines.

5 Add the bottom of his costume and a V-shaped belt at the waist. Draw the legs by adding curves at the knees and the calves. Draw a wavy line around Goliath's head for his hair.

6 Draw straps on David's top using upside-down Vs. Then add the decoration at the center of his chest using ovals. Add the outline of David's wavy hair. Erase the guide lines.

7 Draw the sword in David's hand. Add the features on his face. Do the same for Goliath. Goliath was a giant, so give him big features. Add wavy lines for Goliath's mustache. Add upside-down V shapes to show David's sandals.

8 Shade your drawing of Verrocchio's *David*. Notice that the sculpture is made with a very dark material, so a lot of shading might be necessary to make it look just right.

37

Villa Rotunda

A villa is a large house. A rotunda is a round building, usually covered by a dome, or curved roof. That's how the Villa Rotunda, outside the town of Vicenza just west of Venice, got its name. The house was built to be a circle inside a square. The circle is actually a big, round room with a dome on top. This room is in the center of a larger square that is the same on all four sides. Each side of the square has a porch with stairs. The stairs lead to a tall row of six columns that support the roof. An entrance on each side leads through a short hallway to the circular main room.

Andrea Palladio designed Villa Rotunda in the late 1500s. As a leading architect of the Italian Renaissance, he had a classical style that was copied in buildings around the world.

1

_____

Begin with a horizontal line.

2

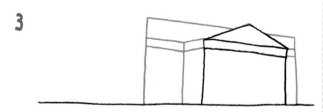

Next draw a house shape. Notice how the horizontal lines slant down to the right a bit. This is the entrance to the building.

3

Add vertical and horizontal lines to each side and to the back of your original house shape.

4

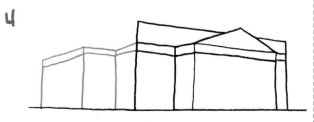

Add three additional rectangular sections on the left. Notice that each section has a line near the top.

5

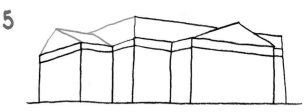

Add a triangular roof to the house. Use two lines to show its depth. Connect this roof to the house with a straight line.

6

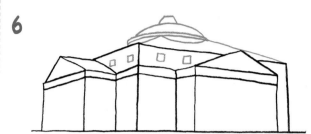

Add square windows. Draw two diagonal lines slanting toward a dome on top. Connect them with a curved line. The dome is made using curved lines. On top of the dome is a small shape.

7

Add rectangular windows with triangles on top. Add arched windows. Draw two rows of columns on the front and the side of the villa.

8

Shade your drawing. Notice the shadows which are dark areas behind the rows of columns. Add tiny vertical lines to show where there are decorative sculptures on the villa.

39

Gondola

Venice is a city made of about 120 small islands. It is only about 3 feet (1.9 m) above sea level. It has 200 canals, or waterways, joined by 400 tiny bridges and a maze of streets. Instead of using cars, most people get around on foot or by boat. Some of those boats are gondolas. Gondolas were invented in the eleventh century. These slim, flat-bottomed boats are guided by usually only one man, called a gondolier. The gondolier stands in the boat and uses a long oar to push it through the water. Because there is usually only one gondolier per boat, the bow, or the front of the boat, curves a little to the left to keep the boat from going in circles. In the sixteenth century, 10,000 gondolas were in use. Today 400 remain.

1

Begin with a flat, wide curving line.

2

Add the top curve and the small bend at the left side of the gondola.

3

Draw tiny lines on the left side of the boat. Add the basic shapes of two people. Use circles for their heads, and curving and diagonal lines for their bodies.

4

Add two more people near the back of the boat.

5

Draw one of the gondoliers at the back to steer the boat. Use a circle and some curved lines for his body.

6

Add the poles that help the men to steer the gondola. Add lines to show the water. Add detail and shade your drawing.

Palazzo Vecchio

The word *palazzo* means "palace" in Italian. The name Palazzo Vecchio means "old palace." It was once the most important government building in Florence, Italy. Signoria is the name of the city's government, so the building is also called Palazzo della Signoria. Since 1872, it has been the town hall. Royalty, such as Duke Cosimo I and the Medici family, who ruled Florence from the fifteenth through the eighteenth centuries, have made the palace their home.

Master builder Arnolfo di Cambio constructed the building from 1299 to 1302. The final touch was a huge bell placed in the 308-foot (94-m) tower. The bell rang to call people to meetings or to warn them of danger, such as a fire or an attack. Famous prisoners were also kept in a tiny room at the top of the tower, called the "little hotel."

1 Begin to draw the main rooftop of the Palazzo with two rectangles. Add lines that extend below them.

2 Next draw two tall rectangles. Notice that one is thin.

3 Begin the lower part of the tower with shapes that become wider at the top. Next add a square and a rectangle above this.

4 Add another tall section to the tower by drawing more rectangles.

5 Draw battlements, the little square cuts that were made into the tower walls so that guards could watch or shoot enemies. On the top tower, draw a triangle with a tiny line and a circle.

6 Erase extra lines around the battlements. Add more battlements on the lower section of the building. Add small lines for windows, and draw arches on both sides of the tower.

7 Add a line for decoration, as shown, below the battlements. Draw windows on both sides.

8 Shade the building, and use criss-crossing lines to show detail.

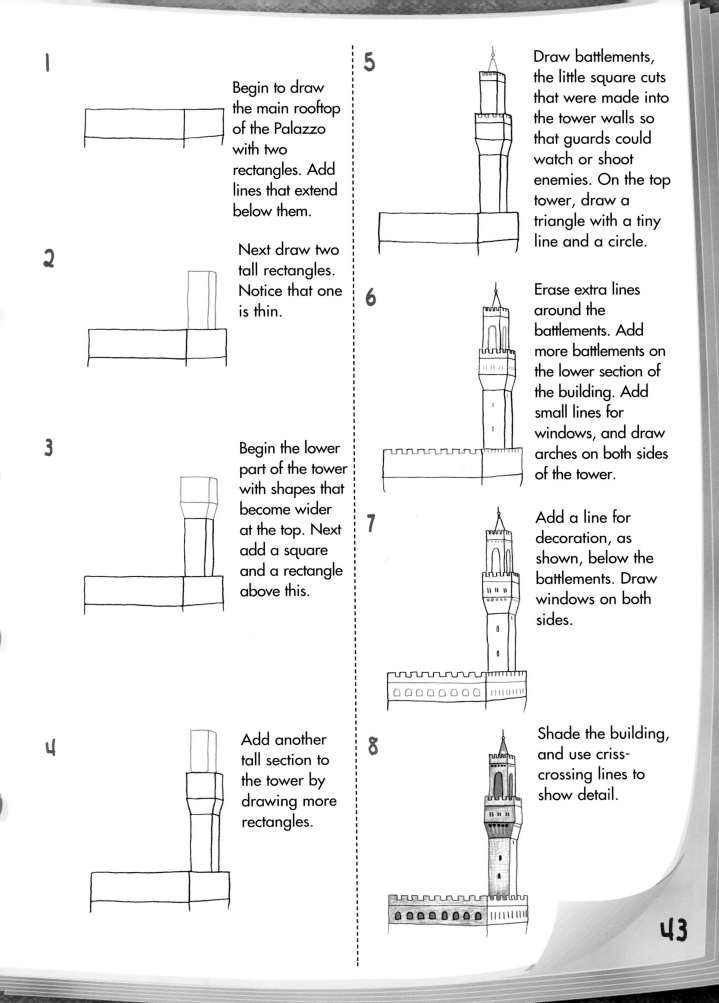

Timeline

3000 B.C.	Greeks formed city Poseidonia.
1000 B.C.	Etruscans settle in southern Italy.
509 B.C.	The Roman Republic is founded.
250 B.C.	Rome begins to build a vast empire.
A.D. 117	The Roman Empire stretches from Great Britain to the Red Sea.
A.D. 330	Constantine builds a new capital at Constantinople.
A.D. 476	Rome falls, and the Pope takes the power once held by the Roman emperors.
1500s	The Renaissance flourishes.
1861	The Kingdom of Italy is started.
1915	Italy enters World War I.
1922	Benito Mussolini becomes head of Italy.
1936	Italy joins with Germany in World War II.
1946	The Republic of Italy is founded.
1957	The Treaty of Rome is signed by six nations, establishing the European Economic Community.
1999	Italy launches the euro as the official currency.

Italy Fact List

Official Name	Italian Republic
Area	116,305 square miles (301,228.6 sq km)
Continent	Europe
Population	57,679,825
Capital	Rome
Most Populated City	Rome, population 2,600,000
Industries	Tourism, clothing, machinery, iron and steel, motor vehicles
Agriculture	Grapes, olives, grain, sugar beets, potatoes
National Anthem	"Fratelli d'Italia" ("Brothers of Italy")
Official Language	Italian
Common Phrase	"Ciao" ("hello" or "good-bye")
Currency	Euro
National Holiday	Anniversary of the Republic, June 2
Favorite Sport	Soccer
Longest River	Po River, 405 miles (651.8 km)
Major Lake	Lake Garda, 143 square miles (370.4 sq km)
Highest Peak	Mont Blanc, 15,771 feet (4,807 m)

Glossary

arch (ARCH) A frame that curves at the top and makes an opening.

architects (AR-kih-tekts) People who create ideas and plans for a building or an organization.

architecture (AR-kih-tek-cher) The art of creating and making buildings.

astronomer (uh-STRAH-nuh-mer) A person who studies the Sun, the Moon, the planets, and the stars.

basilica (buh-SIH-lih-kuh) An early Christian church building.

cathedral (kuh-THEE-drul) A large church that is run by a bishop.

classical (KLA-sih-kul) Concerned with a general study of the arts and sciences.

coffins (KAH-finz) Boxes that hold dead bodies.

design (dih-ZYN) A decorative pattern.

destintation (des-tih-NAY-shun) A place where a person travels.

detail (DEE-tayl) A small part of something.

dictator (DIK-tay-ter) A person who takes power and has total control over others.

drama (DRAH-muh) A play or a skit.

economy (ih-KAH-nuh-mee) The way a country or business manages its resources.

enslaved (en-SLAYVD) To have been made a slave.

executed (EK-suh-kyoot-ed) Put to death.

fascist (FA-shist) A person who believes in a government in which one person has total power.

gladiator (GLA-dee-ay-tur) A person who fought to the death against other men or animals.

granite (GRA-nit) Melted rock that cooled and hardened beneath Earth's surface.

inspiration (in-spuh-RAY-shun) Powerful, moving guidance.

mineral (MIH-ner-ul) A natural element that is not an animal, plant, or other living thing.

monarchy (MAH-nar-kee) A government run by a king or queen.

preserved (prih-ZURVD) To have kept something from being lost or from going bad.

prime minister (PRYM MIH-nih-ster) The leader of a government.

professional (pruh-FEH-shuh-nul) Someone who is paid for what they do.

Renaissance (REH-nuh-sons) The period in Europe that began in Italy in the fourteenth century and lasted into the seventeenth century, during which art and learning flourished.

republic (ree-PUB-lik) A form of government in which the people elect leaders to run the government.

resources (REE-sors-es) Supplies or sources of energy or useful materials.

scorpion (skor-PEE-un) A small animal that has a poisonous sting in its tail.

sculptor (SKULP-tur) A person who makes art by shaping or carving material such as clay or marble.

sculpture (SKULP-cher) A figure that is carved or formed.

symbols (SIM-bulz) Objects or pictures that stand for something else.

tourism (TUR-ih-zem) A business that deals with people who travel for pleasure.

unified (YOO-nih-fyd) Joined.

World War II (WURLD WOR TOO) A war fought by the United States, Great Britain, France, and Russia against Germany, Japan, and Italy from 1939 to 1945.

Index

Web Sites

Due to the changing nature of Internet links, PowerKids Press has developed an online list of Web sites related to the subject of this book. This site is updated regularly. Please use this link to access the list:
www.powerkidslinks.com/kgdc/italy/